I0493030

# Get Real!
# Planning for Life, Death,
# & Disability
## 5 Steps to Get Organized
## & Take Care of Your Family

**Mark E. Wight**

Attorney at Law

www.idahoestateplanning.com

# Get Real!
# Planning for Life, Death,
# & Disability
5 Steps to Get Organized
& Take Care of Your Family

**ISBN #– 978-1535173315**

**Cover Design – Slanted Communication & Consulting**
**Other image credits – Gerrit Campbell & Jackson Turner**
***Data updated in 2024.**

**Mark E. Wight**
**Idaho Estate Planning**
**www.idahoestateplanning.com**
(208) 939-7658

*To my family –
close and extended –
that help me "Get Real."*

## Disclaimers/Terms of Use

By consulting this guidebook all users understand, acknowledge, and agree to all of the following Disclaimers and Terms of Use.

This publication is for informational purposes only. None of the general legal topics discussed in this publication are to be construed as legal advice and should not be regarded as such. This book is not designed to replace any legal advice by Licensed and Qualified Legal Advisors.

This is an educational publication designed to educate users about legal topics and issues that impact individuals in general. These issues may or may not affect any individuals and if so, may affect individuals differently. The topics discussed in this publication are provided to facilitate your educated and informed discussions with your trusted legal advisor.

The information contained in this publication is believed to be accurate. However, laws, circumstances, and several other unknown factors can render any content contained herein to be unreliable, unusable, and/or inaccurate at any time and without notification.

All users assume full responsibility for outcomes and results from the application of, or reliance on, this material. All users accept full responsibility for consulting qualified legal counsel to discuss this material and their own unique legal concerns, issues and circumstances.

The author, publisher, and any affiliates make no offers, promises, warranties or guarantees of any type to anyone by allowing access to this publication.

# Table of Contents

Disclaimer & Terms of Use ............................................5

An Introduction to Get Real ............................................9

Step 1- Get Real - Why You Need to Have a Plan ....17

Step 2 - Get Motivated – How to Avoid the Worst ..23

Step 3 - Get It Together – What to Plan for ................31

Step 4 - Get Help – The Team to Help You ...............57

Step 5 - Get It Done – What You Need to Do Now ..63

About Mark & Idaho Estate Planning.......................69

References & Resources .................................................77

# *An Introduction to*
# *Get Real*

One of easiest things to do in this world is to ignore the future and not just any future, our own future. While we sit and often predict what will happen to other people, we just aren't very good at predicting what will happen to us. It is easy to dream about our own future, whether this concerns our family, our future financial stability, or our continuing good health.

However, when it comes to making specific plans about our own health concerns years from now or even our own mortality, there is a blind spot the size of Mount Everest that we can't see around.

As difficult as this may be to accept, the statistics are clear: the vast majority of us will die. (OK, all of us are going to die – some just haven't come to terms with that reality yet.) They also tell us that the majority of us will at some point deal with mental or physical disabilities associated with the aging process.

However, despite this reality, somewhere between two-thirds to three-quarters of all who read this don't have a written estate plan, in case of death. Even fewer have a written plan in case of incapacity.

The purpose of this book is not to understand why we can't seem to plan. Rather, this effort is to help explain what happens if we don't plan and what we can do about it.

## "Getting Real"

This book is designed to be different than any other book you might have seen about estate planning. The problem for most folks when it comes to estate planning is that they dance around the issues, delay addressing the issues, and often act as if not thinking about the issues will somehow prevent or at least delay their occurrence. So, this book is about **getting real**.

I would like to help you and your family to get the facts that you need to build a solid plan. Then I will explain what issues you need to plan for. I will outline the help you will need to get your plan in place. And then finally, I'll make it super clear and easy for you to know what to do to get it going. So, let's **get real** about how to get your estate plan in order, for you and your family.

The first reality that needs to be faced is simply: life is going to happen to you. I often share with families, especially those who have been in one of my estate planning workshops: that most of us lie to ourselves and stay blissfully ignorant about aging. But even as we ignore it, the clock keeps ticking and we keep aging. In turn, each day as we age, our risks *increase* and our options *decrease*. So, the longer you wait to take action and put a plan in place to protect yourself and your family, the greater the risk of not being able to take any action.

Of course, this begs the question, why do you need to take action and create a plan in the first place? In the upcoming chapters, I will explain in detail what you specifically need to plan for. But here I would like to give you a general picture of reality and what the primary reasons are for taking action and getting your estate in order.

Before I do, it is important to first explain that if you think you already have an estate plan in place, and you set it up even a few years ago, your plan is probably inadequate. And if you prepared your plan five or more years ago, the risk is even greater that your plan won't deliver the outcome you hope it will.

Here's why: having a will or a trust that you set up years ago is more than likely no longer relevant or effective in your situation. If there have been any changes in your life since you created your plan and prepared your documents, then it is very likely that it won't measure up.

New kids, new marriages, new divorces, changes in property ownership, and medical issues for you, your spouse, and any of your heirs/beneficiaries, will change the game.

Also, any changes in the way you title the ownership of your assets, or beneficiary designations, will also impact your plan's effectiveness. And your "plan" is not your documents. Having a will or, a trust, isn't a plan. A plan is your comprehensive strategy to minimize risks, tax exposure, etc. and maximize your estate preservation for your eldercare needs and for your beneficiaries. A will and a trust are tools that can be used to achieve your estate planning objectives.

To be assured that your wishes and preferences are followed if you become incapacitated or die, you need to document your wishes and structure your plan to facilitate those wishes. Then you need to follow a plan for consistent reviewing and improving.

Every plan must continue to evolve to reflect all of the changes in your life and in your heirs/beneficiaries' lives. Failure to keep your plan current with the changes in your life will cause your plan to fail you and those that you love.

For those who don't have a plan yet (remember having a will is NOT a plan) you need to **get real** and get started. You are not going to live forever. Your health will continue to deteriorate as time goes by until you need care either at home or in a facility. And then you will die.

While some do acknowledge that they may need some care in the future, very few **get real** about the amount of time they may need the care and the incredible cost of that care. And although most families understand that Mom and Dad's assets are for their care, they are so often blindsided by how quickly those assets are depleted and Mom and Dad are left with nothing, even when additional and constant care is still needed.

## Understanding Your Family

When it is all said and done, it's the family you're planning for in the first place – whether to help you when you need the care or to enjoy a portion of your estate as you had hoped for. Therefore, in order to plan properly, first you need to understand your family. Proper planning ought to include a detailed discussion of these issues before you make your final decisions. Communication is key.

A proper estate plan most importantly ensures and provides detailed, clear, comprehensive, and customized instructions for handling your affairs in times of mental disability or death. A proper plan coordinates beneficiary designations for your life insurance and retirement accounts to maximize plan benefits in accordance with your goals.

I explain to clients that proper planning starts with a thorough understanding of your needs, goals, dreams, and aspirations. It takes into account your values not just your valuables. It starts with a thorough understanding of your family – those who you care about and who will someday receive the benefits of your success.

I often remind clients that good planning is no accident. However, the lack of planning is an accident waiting to happen. This is the reality. You need to create a plan. It needs to be a good plan. And you need to make sure that it reflects your wishes. And the plan must evolve to reflect the various changes in your life and in the lives of your beneficiaries.

# *Get Real*

# Step One – Get Real:
# Why You Need to Have a Plan

Before we go much further, I want to share a secret with you. I want you to realize that you, and everyone else, already have an "estate plan." Yes, that is what I meant to say. Everyone, including you, already has an estate plan that outlines the terms for what will happen at their death, incapacity, and for their long-term care. You don't need to do anything more to have a plan. However, before you quit reading and place your bet on the plan you already have, you should understand a bit more about this plan and what the options are.

In reality, there are only two types of plans. One type of plan is the one that you get by *design*. You make decisions and choices based on your preferences, resources, and needs. The other type of plan is the one that you get by *default*. This one is the government plan. The government plan is what the government has decided will be the course of action if you are incapable of handling your own affairs or if you need extended medical or nursing care, and then what will happen to your assets when you die.

The "get real" reality check question here is: "why do I need to design a plan if I already have the default plan, (even though it *is* the government plan)?" The quick answer, of course, is that the default government plan, is just designed to "process" you in some efficient and routine way. It is not influenced by your true needs or individual preferences. When you choose to NOT declare your wishes, you become just another burden for the government to manage.

Those familiar with how the government operates will realize that the government does not handle differences among people very well. So, the government will tend to "process" everyone in a similar way. Thus, you will be subjected to the default "estate plan" – a plan that will be indifferent to any of your wishes, goals, preferences, or personal needs. But, don't worry; you'll be treated just like everyone else!

So, it couldn't be easier. For Idaho residents, to use the default estate plan (that Idaho created in 1974 – over 50 years ago) to determine what happens to you and your estate, all you have to do is nothing! Of course, this is what most people do anyway – nothing.

However, by enormous contrast, the plan that YOU design is all about you and your specific wishes and needs. This is the plan I alluded to in the last chapter. With your own plan you are in control of what events trigger certain actions. You choose the people who will step in to manage your affairs when you cannot. You decide what your managers can do and when they can do it. Your plan is all about your needs, your wishes, and your preferences. Each individually designed estate plan is just as unique as the individual whose needs are being addressed. The options are almost endless.

We will cover the two types of estate plans (the default plan versus the designed plan) in greater detail later. But first let's cover some issues and terms that often cause confusion. It's extremely easy to get confused about planning, whether it's estate planning or long-term planning.

## Estate Planning

"Estate planning" refers to planning to control the distribution of your estate – your assets, i.e. your house or other real property, and cash assets such as bank accounts and investment accounts, etc., at your death. Many, many people believe that they do not have an estate. Perhaps thinking of the large plantations of the south or simply someone with a lot of wealth, they do not understand that an estate needn't be very large. In fact, whatever stuff you have in your name at your death *is* your estate.

Estate planning also includes planning for the control or disposition of those assets if you become incapacitated and unable to make your own decisions.

## Elder Law or Long-Term Care Planning

"Elder law" or long-term care planning refers to the types of issues that arise from aging and concerns not only the control or disposition of assets if you become incapacitated, but how you will pay for care when you can no longer care for yourself due to age or incapacity. Estate planning most often centers on how to take care of **others** – loved ones – if you die prematurely while long-term care planning centers on how to take care of **you**, usually in a compromised state, for as long as you are alive.

The challenges of these two areas of concern present a profound contrast. Most often for estate planning purposes, the concern is if you die too soon. For Elder law issues and long term-care planning, (and here's where we **get real** again) the challenge is if you live too long. Both scenarios present important challenges that must be managed. Again, they can be managed by the government's default plan (*no work* on your part) or managed by your own designed plan (*real work* on your part).

Because the line between the need for "estate planning" and the need for "long-term care planning" is neither a bright line nor fixed in the same place for everyone, and because the tools used for both are almost identical, Idaho Estate Planning has coined the term "**Legal Life Plan. ™**"

A **Legal Life Plan™** meshes the provisions of estate planning and long-term care planning and allows our clients to smoothly transition from one stage of life to the other with a plan that evolves over time to meet their changing needs. You will find the term "**Legal Life Plan™**" used in this book to represent a comprehensive overall plan to protect you, your loved ones and your assets.

# *Get Motivated*

# Step Two – Get Motivated
## How to Avoid the Worst

Once you have come to accept that you won't enjoy good health (or life) forever, you can start taking the steps to ensure your needs and wishes are met. Let's talk about changing your attitude about the future and how you can take control with some available tools.

As explained in the last section, there is a huge difference between the two types of plans – *default vs. design*. When you design a plan, you sit down and anticipate future issues concerning your family, your finances, your health, and your long-term care (getting real). That is, you stay in control. You choose what you want to accomplish. You choose which people will step in to help you accomplish your goals. You choose what they will do and when they will do it. The options available to you in designing your plan are almost endless.

One great result of you designing your own plan is how you can control the cost of creating and implementing the plan. When you don't just turn the implementation over to unknown people, you remain in control. The plan you get by default doesn't give you the same control.

As described, the default plan is often called the "government" plan. State legislatures have attempted for some time to come up with a way to:

1) distribute assets in the absence of will,

2) identify and authorize someone to act on behalf of an incapacitated individual when one isn't identified, and finally,

3) provide a way to pay for nursing care when an individual runs out of money or hasn't made other plans.

As a result, governments (both federal and state) have created a "death plan," an "incapacity plan," and a "long-term care plan" as defaults for those who have chosen to NOT design their own plans.

## THE DEFAULT DEATH PLAN
**(Intestate Probate)**

The intestate provisions of the uniform probate code set out the terms of your default will. Under these provisions, at your death, your share of community property goes to your spouse. Separate property is divided 50/50 between your surviving spouse and your children. These code provisions also determine the priority order for appointing a personal representative (formerly known as the executor). Your spouse has first priority, then your children (in no particular order), then your parents.

While the intestate provisions mirrored what many people created in their own wills (or would have), it is clear that the overall concept is limited to those situations where husband and wife were the original spouses (no remarriages) and all of the children are the children of those same spouses. In the early 70s when these provisions were drafted and adopted, this scenario reflected a huge portion of the population. That has changed dramatically in the 50 plus years since then, as the divorce rate has climbed to over 50% of all marriages.

Those same provisions that worked fairly well with spouses in the first marriage don't work well at all in second marriages or blended families. For instance, let's take the situation where a husband divorces then re-marries. We'll assume that he has children from his first marriage (not an unreal assumption) and his new wife has children from her first marriage (again, very common). At his death, his community property with the new wife is now all hers. Any separate property is split between his children and new wife, children sharing 50% and wife taking 50%.

Now the new wife has all the community property and half of his separate property. This may be OK for the husband at least until something happens to the new wife. At her passing, everything that went to her now goes to *her* children, none to *his*. So, with the government plan, he has disinherited his own children and has made his stepchildren his heirs – a result that is almost never what he had in mind. In fact, this is almost always a disastrous result. This is just **one** scenario that needs to be planned for. There are numerous others that are as unique as the dynamics of each individual family, each one nearly as poorly handled by the default plan as this one.

# THE DEFAULT INCAPACITY PLAN
## (Guardianship & Conservatorship)

The probate code does a similar thing with appointing fiduciaries for someone who becomes incapacitated but hasn't previously chosen a fiduciary. A fiduciary is someone who has a statutory duty to care for another or for that person's assets. For example, a guardian can be appointed for an incapacitated person to help take care of him or her, and to help make medical or personal care decisions.

A conservator can be appointed to help an incapacitated person, as to financial or business matters. But the process for either one is quite involved and requires a determination of incapacity, a hearing process to consider who should be appointed, and why, as well as the ongoing jurisdiction of the court to receive annual accountings and reports concerning the protected person. Or, in simpler terms, a lot of red tape.

It can take several weeks to several months to complete the court proceedings, which typically involve a doctor or two, two or more attorneys, and one or more social workers. Notice of the court proceedings must be provided to every interested person. The cost of these proceedings runs from a few thousand dollars to incredible amounts. I recently heard of one situation where the combined legal fees actually exceeded $1 million. This was a rare case concerning a large estate; however, the issues are the same.

## THE DEFAULT LONG-TERM CARE PLAN
## (Medicaid)

If you run out of money to take care of yourself in an assisted living or skilled nursing facility, or at home with the help of others, the government has a program for you. Medicaid is the most common program for paying long-term care costs. The cost for the default or government plan is incredibly high. The cost is simply **everything you own**. Actually, the asset limit is $2000. Everything else must be spent before you are eligible for the government plan.

In addition, all but $40 of your income goes to cover the cost of care. Any incidentals must be paid from the $40 personal needs allowance. If you had in mind to pass assets to your kids, you'll be disappointed. In fact, if you have a house or other "non-countable" assets when you qualify for Medicaid, the state agency administering Medicaid will file a claim in the probate of your estate to recover the equivalent value of any Medicaid payments made on your behalf. So, either way — if you spend down before you qualify or if you maintain some assets when you qualify — at death your estate will be depleted.

## LACK OF FORESIGHT = LACK OF CONTROL
The common element in all of these situations is that the government had to do something. Usually due to the lack of foresight on the part of the person to be taken care of, since nothing was in place and no instructions were left.

Another common element in the default plan is the complete lack of control by the person to be taken care of. The legislature created the plan and dictated most (if not all) of the details. There is very little room for you to be treated or "processed" differently.

The best way to summarize all the bad news about the default or the government plan and what it would mean for you, is: it's expensive, time-consuming, inaccurate, and inappropriate for most of your needs. But here's the good news: YOU DON'T NEED TO USE THESE PLANS. You can create your own!

The Beatles sang, "All you need is love." In terms of estate or elder law planning, you absolutely need love, but you also need a little more. As noted above, you need to realize that you're not here forever and during the time you are here, you will likely experience a period of time with declining physical or cognitive health or both. And finally, you need to realize that whatever you currently have in place for estate planning, more than likely is now inadequate.

Now is the time to make that change in attitude and spend the time and energy to protect yourself, your loved ones, and your estate. So, let's **get real** about what you need to plan for - if you want a designed plan that truly serves your needs and wishes.

# *Get It Together*

# *Step Three – Get It Together*
# *What to Plan For*

At this point, I am certain, at least I hope, you have decided that using the default plan is not an option for you and you are prepared to design your own plan. If you already have a basic plan started, or an old plan, you may be ready to make sure it is up to date and correctly designed to achieve your objectives.

If this is the case, it's time for you to "get it together." This is the process of getting a clear understanding of what is important to you and what you need to prepare for. Your own designed plan needs to be based on strategies that will achieve your objectives, prepare for challenges, provide for your elder care, protect your estate, and protect your family. Once we have a clear understanding of exactly what you need and want to happen, during your lifetime and after, we can design a plan to achieve your objectives.

As noted above, the first goals of any quality estate or elder law plan are to:

1. Protect you and your loved ones during your lifetime, especially in the case of incapacity.

2. Transition your assets to your heirs/beneficiaries with the least amount of hassle and time at the least overall cost to you and your family; and,

3.  Protect your legacy, even a legacy of values and
    not necessarily valuables.

Each of these three core areas: your remaining lifetime,
your death, and your legacy present numerous
challenges, issues, and considerations. Sometimes, clients
do not realize the situations they need to prepare for until
our team brings it to their attention. So, before I hit you
with some facts and a lot of "what ifs" I want you to
know two very important things:

> **First**, once you get an idea of just some of the
> challenges and issues you need to plan and prepare
> for, it could be enough to make you dizzy.
> Sometimes people are so overwhelmed by the
> thought of the decisions they must make, that they
> choose to do nothing at all – which is the worst
> thing to do. If you fail to make your own choices
> and decisions, guess who makes them for you?
> You got it! That puts you back on that
> "government" plan.

> **Second,** this is the work that I do. Every day, I help
> clients to prepare for the future and to protect their
> estate and their beneficiaries. You can't imagine the
> range of family situations I've seen during my 30+
> years of practice. So, what I want you to know is
> that even if this section makes you feel like you
> don't know where to begin, I am here to help you. I
> am here to guide you through the maze and help
> you focus on the decisions that must be made,
> using the most efficient and effective strategies to
> get your estate plan in order. In other words, with

my expertise and experience, I am going to make this process as easy as possible for you.

Okay. It is time for the "what ifs" that you should consider. Let's start with some "warm-up" questions to get you thinking about your specific family needs and issues.

- Who are the people close to you that you're planning for?
- What's their situation?
- Is there anyone with special needs?
- Are any of your children in a less than stable marriage?
- Do you want to protect your spouse from losing everything to nursing home costs?
- Are you a blended family?
- What about protecting your children from a parent's remarriage?
- Have you thought about who would be the guardian for your kids? (If this question alone has you conflicted, we can help you figure this out – so stay focused on the big planning picture.)
- Who would you trust to make decisions for your kids?
- Who do you want to make decisions for you?

No doubt these questions have you worrying that there's so much to think about. Remember, we've done this before, so we have systems in place to help you determine the issues, focus on preferred outcomes, and then prepare a strategy to achieve those desired outcomes.

Your biggest challenge is to be honest and realistic with yourself. You need to consider the way your family is now and how things can change. When you are realistic about the "what ifs," we can design a better plan to protect you and your beneficiaries.

## During Your Lifetime

During your lifetime, it is important to plan for how to handle any future medical challenges or incapacity. This includes a medical/health directive (also called a living will or a medical power of attorney) that indicates who should make medical decisions about your care if you are unable to do so. It is also important that your wishes are clearly stated with regard to what treatments you would refuse and to what extent you want life-sustaining support. It is also necessary for you to discuss your wishes with your designated health care agent to be sure they understand and will follow your wishes.

This isn't just a matter of making sure your wishes are followed though. It is about your privacy. If you don't choose who will handle your health and financial affairs

(If you are unable to), then the government plan kicks in to appoint a guardian. Your business, previously private, now becomes public.

Incapacity and the need for extended nursing care is a major elder care issue. One in nine (11%) of those 65 and older will experience Alzheimer's or some other form of dementia. Even if you personally are not affected, it could be your parents, your in-laws, or your spouse. In one way or another, we are all impacted by the hazards of aging.

Caregiving is a loving but difficult experience. Generally, women are most impacted by the obligations of caregiving. Often wives and daughters take on burdens of care that could be delegated to professionals in elder care. They often assume these tasks as cost saving measures. This is a huge reason for effective pre-planning.

According to government estimates[i], 70% of those turning 65 can expect to need some amount of long-term care during their lives. This means you can't ignore this reality and hope it doesn't happen to you or your spouse. You need to **get real** and plan ahead.

Some questions you should ponder:

- Who is available to help take care of you if necessary?
- Where will you live if you require special care and assistance?
- Would you be able to live at home?

- Would one of your children be able to move in to help you?
- Would you be able to move in with one of your kids?
- Is there an assisted-living facility that would be available to you?
- What if you needed around the clock professional nursing care?
- What will your care cost and can you afford it?

Beyond the reality of needing long-term care, the most shocking issue for many is **the cost** of that long-term care. Some assume that Medicare will cover these costs. However, Medicare does NOT cover long-term nursing care. Medicare will cover up to 90 days of rehabilitation or "acute care," but not long-term care after that. So, payment must come from other sources. More on this in a bit—first let's review the actual costs you can expect.

The average costs of different levels of care[ii] are all staggering. For example:

- Adult day care averages $96 per day.
- Non-skilled in-home caregivers who help to watch over and provide housekeeping and companion care average $35 per hour.
- Monthly rent in an assisted-living facility averages over $5,000.
- Monthly expenses in a nursing home average well over $10,486 per month and up to $15,208 per month.

So how will you pay for any long-term care that is needed by you and/or your spouse?

There are generally four sources of funding to help pay for the significant cost of long-term care. They include:

1.  Self-pay. If you have adequate funds to cover the costs of quality care, you may assume the full cost by using your own assets.

2.  Insurance is another source of funds. Long-term care (LTC) insurance is an option to pay for future required care. The obvious key is to get a policy BEFORE you need it. The longer you wait, the more it will cost and the fewer options that will be available to you. LTC insurance is expensive, and you don't get your money back if you don't use it.

    Another insurance option is whole life insurance with accelerated benefits. These are policies with riders that allow you to access (while you are still alive) a portion of the face value of your life policy due to a disability, terminal illness, or other serious medical problems. This way your premiums are not wasted, and you have more flexibility about how to use the funds. You can use the funds to pay for your long-term care.

3.  Medicaid. Medicaid is the government plan. Medicaid planning is where a lot of people make mistakes. More on this later.

4.  Veterans may qualify for some programs that offer financial assistance to cover special care needs.

## Self-Pay

For some families, there are definitely adequate resources to cover the costs of nursing care. However, you need to do the math. A nursing home at an average of $10,486 per month would be over $125,000 per year. That's every year until you die. If you had any intention of leaving your estate to your beneficiaries, this is a huge amount (that will likely increase every year) that will leave your estate every year. So even if this is something you can afford, it is a good idea to evaluate your options for alternative payment sources.

## Insurance

Long-term care (LTC) insurance is a prudent alternative to help pay for care. Keep in mind that the older and the sicker you get the more LTC insurance will cost you. In fact, you may reach a point where you no longer qualify. This is one of those areas where you need to get moving before you no longer have this option.

LTC insurance premiums are generally very high. I know the description "very high" is relative but expect to have a bit of "sticker shock" when you request a quote. This is of course because the likelihood you will be using it is high. However, the real sticker shock is getting the nursing home bill. Sometimes, clients complain that if they don't need it, (they are the lucky ones who don't need care before they die), that's a lot of premium dollars down the drain. If you think of it like your homeowner's or auto insurance, as a necessary protection from a potentially devastating event, then the costs are a reasonable expense.

When shopping for long-term care insurance, be sure to clarify what will be covered, when it will be covered, and for how long. Be sure that you can afford the costs during any waiting periods before benefits start. Eligibility for benefits can be confusing, so be sure that all of that is spelled out and clear.

Life insurance is also worth mentioning again. A whole life policy with illness acceleration riders can do the following:

1. Provide your beneficiaries with a lump sum inheritance, and funds to pay any estate taxes when you die.

2. Provide you with access to your cash value to fund emergency needs.

3. Provide living benefits by allowing you to access some of the face value of the policy while you are alive or when you have a diagnosed condition or disability that triggers the acceleration. This could give you access to funds to cover long-term nursing care or for anything you choose.

## Medicaid

As I already mentioned, Medicaid is one area of estate planning where families make some big mistakes. Generally, Medicaid is regarded as the government plan – the payer of last resort. There are both clinical and financial requirements for eligibility. And they differ if you are single or married. There are very strict rules about the transfer of assets (that is giving your assets to your kids, etc.) so you can qualify. The wrong timing can trigger a penalty period or ineligibility.

Have you ever seen an infomercial where the actors announce the "don't try this at home" warning? Well, Medicaid planning is one of those areas where you should not make any decisions without the advice of an experienced estate planning attorney. This means, you should not listen to Cousin Bill or Aunt Mary. Even if they tell you that they know exactly what needs to be done to qualify for Medicaid, they probably don't.

Medicaid involves strict guidelines and rules. It is possible to legally qualify and still maintain your estate to pass on to your beneficiaries, but only if everything is coordinated correctly. If you make changes without legal advice, you could subject yourself and your family to huge recovery penalties and also be ineligible for benefits for a penalty period. The key is to get experienced advice and to take action now. Every day that you postpone this part of planning reduces your options significantly.

## Veterans Benefits

Many Veterans are unaware of an obscure benefit that is available to pay additional income that can be used for long-term care expenses. Estimates are that only 1/3 of those who qualify for pension benefits actually apply. The Aid & Attendance[iii] benefit is for wartime Veterans who require the "aid and attendance" of another person or are homebound. Veterans qualify based on wartime military service, extent of care needs, and certain financial qualifications. Surviving spouses may also qualify.

If you or your spouse qualify for benefits under this program, the additional pension could be in the $1,400 to $2,727+ range per month. This could be very helpful in reducing your miscellaneous caregiving and nursing care expenses. Note that financial allowances are adjusted annually.

Helping Veterans has always been a priority for me. I am a Certified Attorney with the Academy of VA Pension Planners and an accredited attorney with the Veterans Administration. So, if you are a Veteran, this will be part of our estate planning discussion. I know how to help Veterans get the benefits they have earned through their greatly appreciated service to our country.

You may also qualify for disability benefits from the VA. The application process is long, confusing, and sometimes frustrating. But if you are eligible and receive a disability benefit, it is well worth the effort to apply.

The secret to receiving a successful award from the VA is not in filling out the forms but in knowing what documents and evidence must be submitted with the application. Knowing the secrets for a successful award – with the special case of long-term care recipients – is 95% of the battle.

## Will or Trust?

I hope you think that this "will or trust" question doesn't make sense. However, many people think that if you have a will, then you have satisfied your estate planning "to do" list. And others think that having a trust means that you no longer need a will. So, the answer to this hypothetical question is that in order to have an effective plan you may need both. Here are some basics that you should know about wills and trusts to help you prepare for a plan that achieves your objectives.

## The Basics About Wills

First, a will is a legal document in which you declare who, at your passing, you would like to receive any assets that you own. Your will (and the subsequent probate process) affects only the assets that are in your name. What many people do not realize is that there are certain types of ownership that override any instructions that you have in a will. This is a mistake people make all too frequently that causes assets to be unevenly divided and not as you intended.

For example: If you have 3 children and you want all of them to split everything equally, then all of the assets must be in your name. Let's assume you have a have a $100,000 savings account and a $200,000 bond that is your name and your oldest child's name, JTWROS (joint tenants with rights of survivorship). When you die, if your will says that all of your assets are to be divided 1/3 to each child, the ownership of the bond will cause an uneven distribution.

The $200,000 bond held JTWROS will go automatically to your oldest outside of the will and probate. The $100,000 that is in your name alone will then get split 3 ways, per the instructions in the will. That leaves your oldest with $200,000 + 1/3 of $100,000, which is $233,333. The other two kids get $33,333 each. This is probably not what you wanted to happen.

This illustrates, among other things, the real need for an attorney: to discuss all of the issues affecting your planning not just to draft documents. In addition, the need to review each asset you own, how's it owned, and what you want to have happen with that asset is critical to a successful estate plan.

Other types of assets and ownership that have overriding beneficiary designations include life insurance and retirement accounts. This is one important reason you should regularly update your beneficiary designations as well as your will to make sure your plan continues to reflect your wishes. A will is not a "set it and forget it" planning tool. It really must be updated regularly to reflect changes in estate planning and tax laws, changes in your family, marriages, divorce, assets bought and sold, etc. This is one of the biggest estate planning mistakes that people make – not keeping their will up to date to reflect their current wishes, assets, issues, and objectives.

Any assets covered in a will go through probate court. You can declare an agent (Personal Representative) of your estate to handle the asset distributions, paperwork with the court, payment of any final debts, etc. The probate process is public, so any of your issues pertaining to your will, creditors, distributions, etc. are all public record. This is one of the reasons that clients also need a trust as part of their plan.

**The Basics About Trusts**

A trust is a legal tool that controls the use, maintenance, and distribution of assets over a period of time. Assets held in the trust's name are private and will not be subject to probate. The trust agreement constitutes the instructions to the "trustee" – a person or entity named to handle affairs when you no longer can or at some other earlier time that you specify. A trust very specifically defines how assets can be invested and maintained as well as how they are to be distributed and when.

A trust achieves a whole variety of estate planning objectives including:

- Privacy – By avoiding probate, your assets, affairs, and beneficiaries remain private.

- Protection of beneficiaries – Assets held in trust can help to protect beneficiaries from predators, creditors, and themselves. Distributing assets immediately in a lump sum to beneficiaries can make them vulnerable in a variety of ways. A trust is especially helpful if your beneficiary is young, in a rocky marriage, has a substance abuse problem, or if they are just bad with money. A trust can specify when and how much can be distributed and to whom.

- Preservation of benefits – Some beneficiaries might be receiving government need-based benefits, such as a child receiving social security disability benefits. An outright inheritance could jeopardize those government benefits. A trust can minimize this risk.

- Protect of assets from remarriages – Trusts can be set up to provide for a spouse while alive and then transfer the assets to the trust maker's children from an earlier marriage. This protects the children from having the trust maker's estate transfer to the new spouse and then the new spouse's children (instead of the trust maker's children) when the spouse dies.

- Removal of assets from your estate – This is a possible strategy to help you qualify for Medicaid while preserving your assets for your beneficiaries.

However, this Medicaid planning requires an experienced estate planning attorney to make sure you understand all of your options and consequences.

Hopefully, this gives you some idea of the variety of ways trusts can be a useful tool in designing an estate plan that serves your needs. In fact, wills and trusts can work in unison to achieve your goals. A will can address any assets that are not yet retitled into the trust account, at the time of death. A will can also be used to create a trust. And for parents of minor children, a will is the tool to declare preferred guardians.

**Choosing Your Agents**

It is important that you choose your agents (executors, trustees, etc.) that are best suited for the task. Sometimes your closest family members are not prepared or qualified to handle the responsibilities that come with being your agent. Be sure you choose those who are willing and able to serve the roles you are asking of them. Make sure your agents understand your wishes and are prepared to follow your directives.

## Funding Your Retirement

One of the key roles of an estate planning specialist is to guide you on the best strategy to maximize your resources to fund your retirement and your elder care needs, while preserving your assets for your beneficiaries. This is an important component of your estate planning. Structuring and accessing your assets in a manner that reduces taxation is also important to your overall asset preservation plan.

## When You Die

When you die, if you have planned properly, your estate distribution should flow exactly as you intended. Your beneficiaries will receive what you have planned for them, when you planned for them to receive it, and in ways that protect them and the assets for generations to come. You will have minimized the taxation of your estate to preserve the maximum amount for your chosen beneficiaries. And you will also pass onto your heirs more than just valuables – perhaps your values or some other priceless legacy.

In order to have this type of outcome, we need to make sure that your plan is designed around your realistic needs and wishes.

**This means we need to plan for:**

- Asset protection – This requires that you maintain appropriate insurance to reduce liability exposure and invest in assets that are in-line with your investment objectives.

- Asset preservation – This requires that you maintain assets in ways that shield them from predators and creditors.

- Tax minimization (income and estate) – This requires that you are always aware of the tax law changes and adjust your portfolio strategy to minimize estate and income taxation. Should you take advantage of the Unlimited Marital Deduction, the Generation Skipping Transfer Tax, or the deceased Spousal Unused exclusion exemption portability allowed to a surviving spouse? Do you know what these concepts are?

- Business protection and succession (if applicable) — This may include creating business entities to shield business assets, a business buyout agreement, or other succession planning to protect your beneficiaries' interests. It may also be important to use care to avoid asset comingling which could put both your personal and business assets in jeopardy of claims against either.

- Beneficiary challenges, issues, and special needs – This requires planning for potential divorces, remarriages, substance abuse, youthful naiveté, bad money management, creditors, predators, special needs, etc.

- Gifting strategy (outright gifts or through a trust administration) – This requires an evaluation of what would be most helpful to the beneficiary and what will help the beneficiary to preserve the assets for future generations. Sometimes the age of the beneficiary is the key influencer about how and when to distribute assets

- Elder care expenses – This requires a solid strategy to cover the costs of any required nursing care, a plan for what resources to use, potential living arrangements, and caregiving plan

- Life insurance – This is a great tool for estate creation, equalization, liquidity, eldercare funding, funeral expenses, estate tax funding, children's maintenance funding, college funding, and much more.

- Legacy objectives – This goes beyond the valuables to include the values you wish to pass onto future generations. These may be meaningful items, family heirlooms, and documented or captured family history that could be priceless for your beneficiaries.

- Charitable legacy – Your planning can include organizations and charities that are important to you.

- Physical care for minor children (if applicable) – This is often a very difficult decision for parents to make. The key is to not let this one area delay your planning. We can guide you with some strategies and ideas to help you make this decision more easily.

- Estate management for minors or children with special needs (if applicable) – This requires that you have a plan and trustee in place to manage the financial matters for your minor children. This doesn't have to be the same person who is the best choice to handle the physical care. For example: Your sister may be perfect to raise the kids but she's bad with money. Your spouse's sister may be the worst choice to raise kids but she's a wiz at money management. This makes it really easy to know who would be best in each role, working in tandem to care for the physical and financial well-being of the kids.

- A pet plan – This is a plan for your "four-legged kids." It is easy to forget that your beloved pets may need a new home if anything happens to you and/or your spouse, so you'll need a plan for who will care for them if anything happens to you.

- Health/medical directives – This requires that you create a living will, also known as a health directive. You should also be certain that your designated representative understands and will honor your wishes regarding medical treatment and life sustaining support.

- Financial power of attorney (POA) – Similar to a medical directive, it focuses instead on your financial affairs. This declares who is authorized to act on your behalf to handle any financial matters if you are unable to. However, some POAs grant authority upon the execution of the document rather than when the subject is incapacitated. So, be sure your POA grants authority when you want it to begin.

- Beneficiary documents – This requires that the beneficiary designations on assets such as life insurance and all retirement related assets and many investment and bank accounts are all up to date and reviewed regularly. It is incredibly easy to forget these once all of the set-up paperwork has been completed and they are maintained on "auto-pilot." This is also the reason so many ex-spouses end up getting that life insurance check instead of the current spouse. Make sure all of your beneficiary declarations are accurate and current.

- Unresolved family disputes – Do you anticipate any disputes once your beneficiaries receive their gifts? Are there any fences that need mending while you still are available to mend them?

- Updated documents – This means they are aligned with current law and your needs and objectives are carefully documented and incorporated into your plan. This may include:

  o will
  o trust agreement
  o health directives (medical power of attorney)
  o financial power of attorney
  o beneficiary declarations
  o insurance policies
  o itemizations of all assets and liabilities and account information
  o safe deposit box and details about larger physical valuables
  o funeral/memorial instructions and family legacy notes and mementos
  o digital assets – usernames and passwords

- Commitment to review and update plan on a regular basis – This requires that you understand the reason why regular reviews and updates must be done on a regular basis. This is about making a commitment to assure that your plan is always accurate and reflective of what you want to occur when you die.

As I warned you, there is a lot to consider when creating a designed plan. But even though it may seem like a bit of work to get your affairs in order, what's worse is leaving all of these important decisions to the government to make on your behalf.

This is where we step in to help you through this process in a thorough and efficient way. We guide you through the best strategies for reallocating assets through trusts or income conversions to allow for the best possible accommodation of assets for beneficiaries thus avoiding or reducing taxes, family disputes and Medicaid penalties. In other words, we identify the best options available to achieve your objectives.

One last note, if you are the adult child of older parents, this is something to bear in mind when seeking to help your parents. It may be difficult for your parents to accept that they need help in the first place. The transition from caring for a child to being cared for by a child is a difficult one. However, if your parents are evading the issues, they may need help more than you realize. And for everyone, this means that proper estate planning should be done earlier, rather than later. The most critical next challenges may be the need for assisted nursing care, especially if there are early signs of cognitive or physical issues.

The most important thing is that you get this taken care of today rather than tomorrow, because everything could change tomorrow, including your available options.

# *Get Help*

# Step Four – Get Help
# The Team to Help You

Sometimes the hardest thing for people to do is to ask for help. Compounding this issue is the reality that over the last few decades, more and more, we are urged to DIY – "do it yourself." Remember when we weren't expected to pump our own gas or put our own furniture together?

And while this trend toward "taking matters into your own hands" has some benefits, in the areas of legal, financial, and health matters it does not. In fact, trying to achieve your legal, financial, and health objectives on your own can often lead to very costly errors and consequences. This is why we strongly urge our clients to realize that in addition to "getting real" and "getting it together" they must also "get help!"

The most effective and successful plans are ones that include guidance of people who are experts in their fields. Would you let your primary doctor perform open-heart surgery on you? Of course not! So, you shouldn't have someone who is NOT an estate planning expert do your estate plan. When it comes to estate planning there are a few experts that will help you to build a plan that addresses your unique issues, challenges, and needs. These experts become your life and legacy team who together help you to maintain your health for as long as possible and to achieve your objectives.

An effective **Legal Life Plan**™ will involve your legal advisor (who specializes in estate planning), financial advisor (who is qualified to manage assets as required by the estate planning process), and health advisors (who specialize in any of your health conditions) among others. It is important that you put your team together so they all can work symbiotically to help you achieve your goals.

**Financial Advisors**

Not all financial advisors are the same. This can be very confusing to clients who are not aware of what the distinctions are among: financial advisor, registered investment advisor, licensed securities representative, financial planner, stockbroker, money manager, etc.

The bottom line is that you need to know what drives your financial advisor's recommendations. How are they compensated? Are they fee-based or do they get paid based on commissions? Do they have any fiduciary responsibility to serve your needs without compromise?

Perhaps most importantly, will they ask appropriate questions and listen carefully to understand what keeps you awake at night, what you would like to achieve in this life and what you would want your loved ones to receive from you? These are important questions to ask as you decide who will be on your team to provide the asset management for your estate.

## Insurance Advisors

During the course of planning your estate and mitigating your risk exposures, insurance may play a significant role. You will need to have access to quality insurance coverage to protect your assets. Insurance can also guard you against liability exposure. Life insurance can play many roles in an estate plan from providing resources for your family when you die to providing resources to fund long-term care expenses while you are alive. Long-term care insurance is an option to specifically address the inordinate cost of assisted living and elder care.

## Health Advisors

Your health advisors not only play a significant role in maintaining your health and managing any medical conditions, but they may also play a role in determining your mental capacity at some point in your life. This will be crucial to when and if your chosen agents will be activated to execute your health directives and financial instructions.

## Legal Advisor

When it comes to a comprehensive estate plan, your legal advisor is somewhat like a team captain. An Estate Planning Legal Advisor is charged with coordinating all of these important advisors so that they function as a unified team working to achieve your objectives and needs for the rest of your life and for your beneficiaries. Each member of the team must realize the consequences of any actions that deviate from your plan. All parties must be committed to serving your intentions, without compromise.

Your legal advisor will guide you through the maze of options and tools which include wills, trusts, health directives, powers of attorney, Medicaid, asset preservation strategies, estate taxes, gifting rules, transition plans, asset transfers, etc. Once you know what you want to happen, it is your legal advisor who will help you to map out a legal strategy, commit the strategy to paper, and then implement it to make it happen.

These are not the type of things that can be accomplished with something you get off the shelf, on the internet, or from a gumball machine. You need to have a team of experts if you want things done correctly. So, part of your comprehensive estate plan requires that you "get help!"

This is where your team of experts helps you to build a **Legal Life Plan™** that works to accomplish your and your family's goals

# *Get It Done*

# *Step Five – Get It Done*
# *What You Need to Do Now*

Throughout this book I have shared with you some of the most important things you need to know to prepare for aging, death, and disability. These can sometimes be very difficult issues to discuss. My hope is that your most important take-away from this book is that you **get real** and **realize** that these things that must get done – and now!

Assume that you know a flood is coming. You realize that you really need to get that flood insurance to protect you and your loved ones and to recover from the inevitable. The problem is that it's too late. Even if you buy that policy today, there's a 30-day waiting period before your coverage kicks in. In other words, by the time the signs are there that you have a situation to deal with, it is nearly always too late to get the help you need to prevent or recover from the damage.

The same thing applies to life insurance. You can't buy life insurance to protect your family when you're dead. You probably can't buy it when you are diagnosed with a life-threatening illness either. So, you need to get protection like this in place – now.

The chances are very high that at some point you may not be able to make medical or financial decisions on your own behalf. You can't choose who will make these decisions for you once things start to fall apart. You need to make these decisions now; when you know exactly what you want, and you are completely competent to grant such authority.

Even when it comes to planning for elder care, waiting to the last minute, or when the need for care is imminent, it is often too late for you to have access to a full range of options. Medicaid planning requires expertise and advance planning.

Every day your risk of illness, injury, incapacity, disability, and death increases and with these risks your options to minimize the impact on your estate decreases. If we wait long enough, then the only options left is those made for us out of desperation. Timing is everything. In order to maintain control as long as possible and to have an effect on your own quality of life decisions you must choose to act now. Your decisions need to be made and documented correctly.

We all want to stay in control of our lives as long as possible and for that we must plan. When it comes to planning for the future, the sad fact is that every day that we fail to plan, we lose options.

The reality is that there isn't a single moment in your life when you're *ready* to plan your estate. You don't just reach some magical "pause button" where everything stops and there's nothing new happening in your life, your business, your investments, or with your loved ones. Likewise, there is no time to stop planning. This is why you need to take action now – because now rather than later really is the perfect time. And taking the right steps now can truly affect your future well-being.

This is why my firm, **Idaho Estate Planning,** created the **Legal Life Plan™** that meshes the provisions of estate planning and long-term care planning and allows our clients to smoothly transition from one stage of life to the other with a plan that evolves over time to meet their changing needs. You will find the term **"Legal Life Plan™"** used in this book to represent a comprehensive overall plan to protect you, your loved ones, and your assets.

Our **Legal Life Plan™** includes annual reviews of the assets contained in your estate plan and any changes made since the previous year review. Regular updates and reviews help to assure that your plan stays perfect – always reflecting the current laws, assets, challenges, issues, needs, and preferences. We help you integrate your financial plan with your legal plan and health plan.

**To ensure a successful Legal Life Plan™ - we will:**

1) educate you and your team.

2) take the time to get to know you, your family, your desires, your concerns, your goals, and your potential problems.

3) gladly and patiently answer questions until you understand the concept or issue; and,

4) based on experience with the problems and results caused by poor planning we have seen over the years, help you design and implement the plan that fits your concerns and goals.

At **Idaho Estate Planning** we have the experience and expertise to help you maintain your options and protect yourself as well as your loved ones now and into the future.

**Once your plan is in place our goal is to make sure:**
- You understand your plan.
- It addresses all of your goals.
- It addresses all of your fears and concerns.
- And, you can finally sleep at night knowing you have a plan designed just for you to address and manage your unique estate concerns.

The time is now to do it right with the right team. We are here to help you plan for the future.

Idaho Estate Planning
**www.idahoestateplanning.com**

Or reach out to a trusted and personally referred estate planning attorney local to your state or city.

# About Mark Wight
# & Idaho Estate Planning

Mark Wight, President, and Founder of Idaho Estate Planning has been practicing law for nearly 40 years, 38 years in the Treasure Valley. He graduated from Utah State University with a Bachelor of Arts in Philosophy and a Bachelor of Science in Environmental Studies. Mark's legal career began in 1985, after he graduated from J. Reuben Clark School of Law, Brigham Young University spending two years at the Department of the Interior in Washington D.C.

Mark is a member of the Idaho State Bar, the Taxation, Probate & Trust Law Section of the Idaho Bar and Wealth Counsel. He is also a certified Adjunct Practice Advisor for Atticus, Inc., a nationally recognized attorney coaching organization. This allows Mark to share his experience and training with other attorneys around the country.

Mark has co-authored several manuals for attorneys in the areas of Probate Administration, Estate and Estate Tax Planning, Medicaid Planning, VA Benefits Planning and Asset Protection. He has taught thousands of hours of education in the areas of estate planning, asset protection, Medicaid and VA benefit planning to other attorneys, CPAs, and financial and health care professionals.

Mark's commitment to education extends to *The Senior Matters Podcast*, where Mark interviews subject-matter experts to help seniors (including those approaching retirement age) and their families and caregivers, navigate issues like long-term care, aging in place, and other living arrangements, estate and financial planning, physical and cognitive health and more. Tune in on your favorite podcast platform or visit www.idahoestateplanning.com/podcast for more information.

Mark and his wife JoAnn reside in Boise and have six children, six grandchildren, and Sadie the golden retriever who has no respect for personal space.

*Scan the QR code to find the Senior Matters Podcast*

*Tune-in anywhere you listen to your podcasts or visit our website at www.idahoestateplanning.com/podcast*

# *What the Team at Idaho Estate Planning Can do for You*

The Idaho Estate Planning team has a combined experience of more than 70 years in the areas of estate planning, asset protection, probate, estate litigation, Medicaid, and VA benefit planning. Because of this experience, we're uniquely qualified to help you avoid the time, hassle and expense of probate, estate litigation, conservatorships, and guardianships.

We have helped nearly 4,000 clients protect themselves, their families, and their legacies through carefully designed and executed plans.

Idaho Estate Planning's legal team is a team you can trust to listen and understand your personal situation, your fears, and your goals. Work with us and we'll put together a Legal Life Plan™ that works for you and your loved ones.

We understand the challenges faced by older Americans, especially Vets, and their families. Over the last five years alone we have helped our clients to received nearly $3 million in care benefits from Medicaid and the VA.

We have a professional network throughout the Treasure Valley and Idaho who are experts in financial and insurance planning, health care, home care, hospice, assisted living, memory care and skilled nursing.

We have the experience and expertise to help you maintain your options and protect yourself as well as your loved ones now and into the future. For more information on elder law and estate planning subjects, contact **Idaho Estate Planning** and schedule a consultation.

**Mark E. Wight**
**Idaho Estate Planning**
www.idahoestateplanning.com
(208) 939-7658

Idaho Estate Planning

SCAN HERE

*Are You Ready to Get Real?*
*Then, Get Real Help!*

*Contact a local estate planning attorney that has*
*been referred to you by a truly trusted and*
*professional source. Idaho residents are invited to*
*contact Idaho Estate Planning.*

*Contact Idaho Estate Planning*
*for a Discovery Right Fit Consultation*

Idaho Estate Planning
www.idahoestateplanning.com
(208) 939-7658

# References

[i] http://longtermcare.gov/the-basics/who-needs-care/
[ii] http://longtermcare.gov/costs-how-to-pay/costs-of-care/
[iii] http://www.benefits.va.gov/pension/aid_attendance_housebound.asp

# Resources

https://www.medicaidplanningassistance.org
https://www.alz.org
https://www.census.gov

Idaho Estate Planning
**www.idahoestateplanning.com**
(208) 939-7658